"Proof..."

First published in the United Kingdom in 2023 by
Shearsman Books
P.O. Box 4239
Swindon
SN3 9FN

Shearsman Books Ltd Registered Office
30–31 St. James Place, Mangotsfield, Bristol BS16 9JB
(this address not for correspondence)

www.shearsman.com

ISBN 978-1-84861-885-5

ACKNOWLEDGEMENTS
The first seven poems in this sequence were first published in
Shearsman magazine; thanks to Kelvin Corcoran.

"Proof…"

Peter Riley

Shearsman Books

Proof that the world exists. Crossing Europe
in the backs of lorries, the noise of the engine,
the road rolling under, deeper by night.
Occasional glimpse of an urban skyline
changing lorries before dawn. Proving
that the world is, but unstable: the Refugee's story.
I usually wake up about four to half past
and don't sleep again until after five.
I lie there listening. And it is through
this hole in the night that the wren sings.

The wren sings a series of single-pitch rows, usually
five to nine notes long, decorated with curlicues.
Some of these "notes" are tight clusters or quick calls
interspersed with short rows of chirps, a slide or two
and finally the "tell-tale machine-gun rattle" which
tells the tale of the Refugee's journey across Europe,
a sonorous black hole day after day.

Doubt that the world will continue. She doesn't
rest long, she flits upstream and perches
on somebody else's ribcage. First light slowly
infiltrates the bushes where the wren lives,
beyond the canal, whispering widths
of hope to the immediate vicinity,
realised currently as white blossom.

How eagerly then my tongue ran off with me
to the far edges of visibility
where the red flower becomes symmetrical
and plunges into the ground. Where
the light traversing the day is refracted down
to the green spread. At a far edge
of urban tension the Refugee
hands over €500 cash to get him from Italy
into Switzerland invisibly.

Half my life I sang in death's anthem
and played death's bones, why should it
bother me now? — always ahead,
inhabiting and sealing the moment in its harmony,
completion and fullness of the world
inscribed on its cist. How do you get mortal harmony
out of a stone box into the moving air?
With ash and ink, and sing a lyric air with passion.

The Refugee in a sleeping-bag on a steel floor
opens his eyes on darkness and wonders
did he remember before he left to visit
the old holm oak up the fields, to hold
its spiked leaf in his hand and listen
to what it said? Go, it said, go now.
I'll be with you, I'll let you know
when we're on the sea.

The vast dark history that trails behind the route,
the great lamentation stretched across the western land-mass
for the fall of Constantinople, Dufay 1454, a version
still sung in Greek villages. And the local text,
for whomsoever is lost. *Whomsoever is here,*
Whomsoever is there, Whomsoever is
everyone you ever cared about
hidden in what's left of the world
where would that be now?

The song thrush arrives and takes up position
in the tall sycamores near the station,
and shouts like the Queen of Night:
filip filip filip codidio codidio
quitquiquit tittit tittittereret tereret tereret
and leaves it there, confident
that the Refugee will get here safely,
the hawks will leave it alone.
The thrush calls *chook chook* just in case
and returns to watching the arrivals at the station.
Not this one maybe next. If not this one maybe next.

The leaves everywhere are a-twitter
with passionate apprehension, summer
heat in April meaning the world is alive
but argumentative. It rattles. Everything:
tongue, toes, teeth, tins they all rattle
society rattles with joy and dole, the lorry
rattles its way across Belgium, crows, water pipes,
windows, Beethoven, they all rattle and shake.
And all this rattling rattles towards us, getting
quieter and faster as it gets nearer until it seems
to enclose us in a gently trembling mist
which is all we know of current world and people.

There may well be world
but there is probably no future. Earth's
moisture sucked into the blue sky,
lost rhymes fallen into dry ditches.
Dreams of belonging, songs of perfect stasis
sung in corners of the Kalahari
where nothing more is asked of earth than
its impetus. The Refugee, parked somewhere,
listens to the total darkness and knows
future is all there can be, to this entire
blackness what can there be but a slow dawn?

A thin line of light along the ridge top
with a door in it. The dark angel
in the left jamb demands a password,
ticket machine gleaming like the moon
as it clicks you into no more than possible life.
Stay there, it says, stay there now, speak
to the old thorn bush on the edge of the allotment
growing from your grandfather's buried skull.

What we know: *Time sets all things right*,
and *It is all for everyone such as there is of it*
and *We do not go, we stop.* Listen to the music
in the sky while the inspector
examines the seal on the tailgate.
Unnoticed, another love-locked innocent
slides over the edge as they do
soul by soul and silently
into nonentity. The last San Bushman
waiting at a corner of perception, the last expert,
the last inspector, an invisible tear
reaching the open lip, and thinking,
"Bliss was it in that dawn to be alive!"

There is no word. The birds have departed,
the trains come and go. We sit in groups
under the stars, in search of
magnyfycence ("...compatible
in Skelton's conception with
magnificentia, a sub-virtue of Fortitude, a virtue
        traditionally held to consist of a measured self-
        control through which one could withstand
        the temptations of both prosperity and adversity."

The hope lost in sixty years of, not social, not
democracy, something else, something that makes
a failure total. Up in the factory zones
we never knew what insidious cruelty dwelt
in privilege until it came at us with a vengeance.
It is our country. God gave it us.
They helped themselves to all of it
and now cheerfully await the outcome nonentity.

Remembering a childhood passed
in grey streets populated by shades.
A shade sells you vegetables, a shade
brings bottles of milk to your doorstep.
A shade dictates mental arithmetic, a shade
works a sausage machine, a shade drills your teeth.
A shade prays. The light passes through them,
they don't cast shadows and mirrors don't reflect them.
A group of shades on the other side of the road
stops and calls me and asks what's my name, what
am I doing here who look so fresh and substantial
and when shall I be on my way.

Mattress on bare boards in the corner.
One of everything: one spoon, one cup,
one bowl, one plate, one ring,
one toothbrush, three Christmas cards.
No heating. Out of the front door at
eight to meet the blaze of snow, returning
at ten with an electric fire and a branch
of holly in berry. Centuries of mutual
aid open before us, make and mend,
beg and borrow, far from home.

At the back of Rochdale there are
bowers of inebriate geology where streams
pass between grassed humps among small trees.
You can't take a car any further, enter a farmyard
and apologetically turn round, careful on the mud.
In these hollows is where they gather
and a hand touches an upper arm gently,
turning to sing in your ear
fortuna desperata or any other
municipal song-sheet. This is where
the troths are plighted, the deals sealed
that will never be broken, dependent
on a courtesy residual in the structure.

Thursday, market-day and again a bird sang,
across the canal, which was frozen over, not a wren.
By Sunday there were three or four. Is this a turn
of the tide, is there hope of something more
than a stray pheromone riding the breeze?
Did something mean something while we
weren't looking? Dark shadows cutting
at the house corners into the snowy fields.
Telling the time by fluctuations of
nightlong traffic, getting heavy
between five and six the whole vessel
riding for a better home, moon after moon.

The night is increasingly a door
opening to let the chorus in, the land
unfolding from its borders.

Robin, fill your little lungs,
and blow your meaning over the fields
fortissimo for the new year.

Be clear and precise, a clarion call
across the solar wind, prelude
to the mass response.

A chorus of slaves, a chorus of prisoners,
a chorus of refugees, singing down
country roads into the town.

The Refugee has sold his office-cleaning business
and bought a horse farm in North Staffordshire
and sits there at night surrounded by the dark hills.
Hidden in their folds are small flickering lights:
refrigerators, slot machines, juke boxes,
all in the process of being switched off.
A cinema organ ca. 1940 changing from
pink to blue sinks and the lid is drawn over.
All these small lights and brief reflections
are sent out like a chorus but tremble, fall,
and are extinguished. A hand gathers the bits
and blows on them too late the dust is hard
in the eyes that made it.

Stay here. There's nothing outside,
nothing left, nowhere to go and nothing to be
except the past. Which comes ready sliced.
It's all been contracted out and dispersed
taking its memory and its pride with it.
I'm talking about Bamako. I'm talking
about Venice. I'm talking about home.

The habitual walk up the lower valley,
patches of balsam and knotweed
surviving where they can,
strength, urgency, storm the airport, return to company.

When the brain sees the promise being fulfilled
it lets us out, and we wander abroad
free of childish panic,
beautifully tensed on the windy earth.

Contrary to planning permission
a room full of light, windows on
three sides looking out on the whole,
on the whole valley. The valley below.

The forgotten books which fill
all the shelves in the house,
warning of the pending war in which
Britain becomes a fascist state by default.

Upper Kentmere, the light passing through
sheets of glass brushes soundlessly against
our turned backs as we sit there trying
to explain why we decided not to follow the world.

And all night the ghosts gritting their voices
on the pages of forgotten books...

There is no photograph, drawing or print that can begin
to show what we are, divided and silent in the lap
of the night wind that rears the sea against the stone
as the red army marches into town.

Or the local Junior Brass Band
marching for its 50th anniversary
to *Lonesome Road* followed by
speeches, quiz, raffle results,
buffet, late disco ends at 11.
            A place on the move
from its nucleus to its periphery
look up look down I never
saw so much darkness, alone
on that road, no one can walk it for you.

Where the station cafeteria spills
onto the platform, I sit and wait.
Small table, chair, coffee in paper cup.
Eastbound trains stop a few metres from me,
the doors open and aware of the gap they
step down into a voiceless assent.

Where is the sky I was promised,
banded in pink and grey and full
of sentence? Will it be towed here?
Will it step down from a parked vehicle
in silken slippers onto the edge
of land and sea, a warm industrial
breeze at our backs that propels us
towards our own long-term home?

Thomas Carlyle of all people.
The Manchester Insurrection: "A million
of hungry operative men, rose all up,
came out into the streets and… *stood there*."
What else could they do? *You own us.*
What do you intend of us, powers, we are
ready to work, and to be shot, if we knew the why."
What is justice? What is truth?
What is daylight?

www.ingramcontent.com/pod-product-compliance
Lightning Source LLC
Chambersburg PA
CBHW021949040426
42448CB00008B/1306